Blockchain & Financial Freedom

3rd Edition

Achieving Wealth and Liberty in the Digital Age

Table of Contents

Notice

This book does not provide financial advice; it is solely intended for informational purposes.

Introduction

What if the most powerful tool for human freedom wasn't a new law, a revolution, or a protest, but a simple line of code?

For almost two decades, I've lived inside the world of software, watching technologies emerge and fade. But when I was introduced to blockchain, I discovered something entirely different. It wasn't just another piece of software; it was a key—a key to a future where you reclaim control.

The people in power do not want you to grasp this. They would prefer you dismiss it as mere "digital money" for niche enthusiasts and for those operating in the shadows.

This is not a technical manual. This is the story of the most transformative idea of the 21st century: Decentralized Trust. It means we no longer need to place our faith in faceless corporations or powerful institutions. Instead, we can trust a system that is open, transparent, and belongs to everyone.

Imagine a world where…

- You truly own your identity and data—not massive social media companies or tech giants.

- You hold your money in your own digital wallet—where no bank can freeze your assets.

- Every agreement is secured by transparent code,

making deception impossible.

This is not a fantasy. It is unfolding now. We will explore how this single idea provides solutions to our most pressing challenges:

- **Taming AI:** How can we prevent a small elite group from monopolizing history's most powerful technology?

- **Ending Digital Manipulation:** How do we dismantle the algorithms that control what you see and shape what you think?

- **Fixing Finance:** How do we create a global economic system that serves everyone, not just the privileged?

- **Enforcing Accountability:** How can we establish absolute transparency, even in matters of war and conflict?

Make no mistake—those in power will attempt to break it. They will attack, regulate, and resist. But we will see what happens in the future.

1. An Introduction to Blockchain

When people hear about Bitcoin, many think about the amazing stories of early investors becoming millionaires. And it's true—blockchain technology, which Bitcoin is built on, can create new financial opportunities.
For example, someone who invested about $1,350 in Bitcoin in 2013 would have seen that investment grow to be worth millions of dollars just a few years later. This growth happened partly because traditional government-issued currencies often lose value over time, making them poor for long-term savings.

But this book is about something much bigger than personal wealth. Its real value can't be measured in money.

Many people see the surface-level story of getting rich but never look deeper. They miss the real point: blockchain is not a one-time chance to make money. It is a tool for lifelong learning and a new kind of freedom.

Like any new technology, blockchain may have weaknesses. Powerful institutions may try to control or limit it. But the **idea** behind it—a system built on open trust—is now permanent. This is an idea that thinkers and philosophers have imagined for centuries. Blockchain is the first real step to making that dream a reality for everyone.

In 2009, an unknown creator named Satoshi Nakamoto introduced Bitcoin. This was more than just a new payment system—it was the solution to a financial problem that has troubled societies for thousands of years. The world is still trying to understand everything it makes possible.

What Is Blockchain?

Blockchain technology is a digital ledger—a record-keeping system—designed to store data securely, transparently, and in a decentralized way. While it was first created for the Bitcoin payment system, its potential uses extend far beyond finance.

When you study blockchain technology, it opens your eyes to new possibilities for autonomy and transparency in many areas of life. It highlights what could be possible in areas like social media, protection from propaganda, and safeguarding against digital manipulation.

The core difference between a centralized and a decentralized system lies in control and transparency. In a centralized system, a small group controls the data, requiring everyone else to trust them. In a decentralized system, like blockchain, individuals can independently verify the data's accuracy for themselves.

Blockchain offers a powerful solution for systems that depend on public trust, such as voting. It can ensure the process is honest and transparent from start to finish. It is notable that no major government has yet adopted blockchain for national elections. This hesitation to embrace a verifiable system underscores a key point: traditional power structures often expect trust without providing proof. In contrast, blockchain empowers people to verify, reducing their need to blindly trust any central authority.

What Problems Does Blockchain Solve?

Learning becomes more efficient when we replace long explanations with a process of asking questions, experimenting, and learning from mistakes without fear. Questions activate our curiosity. When you can't answer a question, you become motivated to find the solution. In contrast, lengthy explanations can easily make a listener lose interest.

In my teaching, I use questions and answers to avoid long lectures. This method makes questioning, trying, and making mistakes a constructive way to master any subject.

As a German philosopher once said:

> What does not kill me makes me stronger.
> *Friedrich Nietzsche*

This logic also applies to making mistakes.

> A mistake that doesn't break you makes you wiser.

Controlling The Financial System

Throughout history, humanity has often moved in a recurring cycle. A group of leaders rises to power and governs society. Over time, systems often become corrupt, losing public support. This frequently leads to revolution, aiming to replace the ruling class.
However, after a system is dismantled, a new group of leaders typically takes power, and the cycle tends to repeat itself. This pattern has kept societies in a closed loop for thousands of years.

A key mechanism that enables a small group to maintain power is control over the economy, specifically through the money system. Historically, gold was chosen as a form of money for several reasons: its scarcity, the effort required to obtain it, and its appeal as a metal.

Yet, throughout the ages, those in power have debased even gold by mixing it with copper to fund wars—a practice known as currency debasement. This involves reducing the precious metal content in coins. It was a common strategy for ancient empires, like the Romans, to finance military campaigns or manage financial shortfalls.

A similar form of this hidden tax continues today, though many people may not recognize it. Modern currency is primarily paper or digital. Governments can create digital money with a few keystrokes, while printing physical money costs only a few cents per note. In essence, authorities can introduce large amounts of currency into circulation.

Creating currency offers significant advantages to authorities for two main reasons:

1. They hold a monopoly on its creation; any competition is severely punished.

2. The production cost is minimal, but the currency can be used at its full face value.

However, creating more currency reduces the purchasing power of the money saved by ordinary people. This phenomenon is called "inflation." Understanding this history is essential for grasping the purpose of Bitcoin—a digital currency built on blockchain technology, designed with a strictly limited supply to resist such manipulation.

There is a quote which states:

> It is well enough that people of the nation do not understand our banking and monetary system, for if they did, I believe there would be a revolution before tomorrow morning.
> *Henry Ford*

I previously explained some of the economic problems of how authorities use control of money to control society. An American politician once said.

> If you control the oil, you control the nations; If you control the food, you control the people; If you control the

> money, you control the world.
> *Henry Kissinger*

Control over the money system is one of the most significant factors that allows authorities to maintain a strong influence over a population, often without the majority of people being fully aware of it.

Consider daily life in most societies around the world. You may find that your job consumes the majority of your waking hours, leaving insufficient time for family and the things you truly value.

> In today's society, people do not work to live but live to work.

Satoshi Nakamoto introduced blockchain technology. Its core idea could mark a turning point for human society, potentially moving us away from systems of concentrated control. In this way, modern forms of economic coercion could become a historical phenomenon for future generations.

If you point a weapon at a person, their answer will be based on your command. However, you cannot intimidate a blockchain, as it has no central point to attack and no individual to pressure.

Many individuals in modern societies believe they have full control over the money in their bank accounts. In reality, the bank holds primary control and can restrict access under certain conditions.

Even if you use cash, its value is not entirely in your control. Central banks can create new currency, and when they do, it reduces the value of all the money in circulation, including the cash in your pocket.

When a government prints currency in excess, it effectively claims a portion of the value that people have worked hard to earn. In economics, this phenomenon is known as the reduction of purchasing power, or inflation.

There is a relevant quote that states:

> Give a man a gun and he can rob a bank. Give a man a bank and he can rob the world.

In most cases, someone who robs a bank is brought to justice. However, those who manipulate the global financial system are rarely held accountable.
Of course, not every person in a position of power is corrupt. However, everyone has vulnerabilities. If someone cannot be persuaded by financial incentives, they might still be influenced by pressure or threats to themselves or those they care about.

Blockchain technology offers a potential solution to this problem by distributing authority instead of centralizing it.

Power is spread across a global network. In fact, anyone can download the blockchain, maintaining a complete and transparent copy of all data and transactions.

Decentralized Payment

A decentralized payment system means there is no central point of control that can be threatened or influenced. The process of creating new bitcoins, known as "mining," relies on a global network of computers competing to solve complex mathematical puzzles. The first computer to solve the puzzle is automatically rewarded with new bitcoin. In Bitcoin's early days, individuals could mine using standard laptops. As network activity grew, the system began to require more powerful, specialized computers to maintain security and process transactions. This process is analogous to the resource-intensive work of mining for gold.

This stands in contrast to traditional monetary systems, where central authorities can create new currency by controlling the banking system. This can dilute the value of the money that people earn through their daily work.

Centralized digital systems grant banks significant authority. They can create digital money and enforce rules on how existing money is used, including monitoring transactions, restricting account access, or limiting where funds can be sent.

In many modern economies, there is a distinction between those who generate value through work and those who manage the monetary system. This dynamic can sometimes create a disconnect between the creation of value and the control of currency.

A key feature of Bitcoin is its limited supply, which is capped at 21 million coins. Nearly 19 million are already in circulation, with the final coin expected to be mined around the year 2141.

In summary, blockchain technology introduces an alternative to traditional financial and social institutions. While mainstream media coverage of cryptocurrencies can sometimes be skeptical, it's valuable to research the technology directly.

For international money transfers, traditional systems involve intermediaries like banks, which often impose limits, fees, and delays. Bitcoin offers a more direct alternative, enabling anyone to send any amount to any country with greater speed and lower fees, requiring only an internet connection and a digital wallet.

It is worth noting that this technology represents a shift in how value is controlled and transferred. While some governments are exploring its adoption—with El Salvador recognizing it as legal tender—others are still determining their approach to its development.

2. Blockchain & Money

At first glance, the question of what money is might seem silly because we all use it daily and assume we know what it is. But the question makes sense if you haven't looked into it. Since blockchain involves payment systems, it's crucial to grasp the concept of money before diving deeper. Understanding the basics of money is vital because we all use it throughout our lives. Once you grasp the concept of money, your perspective can change, which will affect your life's change. Many of us learn about money from our parents, who often work for it and believe they understand it.

A Brief History of Money

In ancient times, people often faced imbalances in their possessions. Consider a man who owned a cow and desired meat, but the animal was too much for his family to consume before it spoiled.

He found others who were willing to share the cow. These individuals took a portion and gave the man a claim check— a promise to repay the value whenever he needed something they possessed. This system of bartering allowed for a fair exchange, ensuring each party received what they needed.

In this way, everyone could share the meal. People began using "IOUs" (short for "I owe you"), keeping these claim checks from friends and trading partners.

An IOU from a major merchant or reliable person was considered more valuable than one from someone less established, as they were more likely to honor the debt.

As societies grew more complex, people often had a surplus of one item but a lack of others. This made a common, trusted unit of value essential. The most reliable IOUs began to function as an early form of currency, with people preferring those from wealthy and trustworthy sources.

However, issuing too many IOUs without the means to repay them leads to instability, as a promise is only as good as the ability to keep it.

These trusted IOUs were the precursors to modern currency. Today, some people trust the U.S. dollar, others the Euro, based on their faith in the issuing government. A currency note itself has negligible intrinsic value; it is merely printed paper costing a few cents to produce.

This leads to a critical question: what happens if a country creates a huge amount of currency that it cannot ultimately back with real value?

An Easy Example of Inflation

Let's simplify how the economic system works. Imagine there is $1000 in circulation in a country, and let's use oranges to represent all the products available. We'll say

there are 1000 oranges for sale.
If each orange costs $1, a person with $3 could afford to buy three oranges.

Now, what happens if the government prints an extra $4000? The total money in circulation becomes $5000, but the number of oranges remains the same—there are still only 1000.

Without most people realizing it, the price of an orange will rise. Now, each orange costs roughly $5. This phenomenon is what economists call **inflation**.

In our example, before the inflation, a person with $3 could buy three oranges. After the inflation, with the price at $5 per orange, that same $3 is not enough to buy even one.

Where did the value go?

So, where did the value go?
The answer is simple: the currency issuer created $4000 out of thin air. With this new money, they can buy 800 of the available oranges. This leaves only 200 oranges for everyone else to buy with the original $1000 they hold.

> By a continuing process of inflation, government can confiscate, secretly and unobserved, an important part of the wealth of their citizens.
> *John Maynard Keynes*

Inflation reduces purchasing power by increasing the amount of currency in circulation.

This creates clear winners and losers. The losers are those who save their wealth in the official currency; the amount of money they have stays the same, but its value decreases, allowing them to purchase less. The winners are those with the authority to create new currency. They can create money at a minimal cost, yet it allows them to claim a share of the economy's real goods and services, effectively drawing value from everyone else's holdings.

Relying on a currency that can be created so easily requires significant trust and carries risk. This is why wealthy individuals often invest millions in assets like real estate, precious metals, and art by famous artists. Unlike currency, these tangible assets are scarce and cannot be duplicated or created from nothing.

A critical question remains: If a government already collects billions in taxes, why does it need to create and release more currency? Perhaps the reason is that this form of "hidden tax" is not widely understood, allowing it to continue without significant public challenge.

> People who don't understand inflation often suffer financial consequences because of it.

How Gold Backing Limits Money Printing?

There is a solution to prevent authorities from printing excessive fiat currency and devaluing it. For years, governments maintained gold reserves to back the currency they issued. Each unit of currency was a claim check redeemable for a specific amount of gold. This system prevented governments from printing more money than they could afford.

Fiat currency

Fiat currency is not backed by a physical commodity like gold or silver. Its value is based solely on trust in the government that issues it and is established by legal decree rather than any intrinsic worth. Ultimately, a fiat currency's value relies on this trust; if the government fails to uphold it, the currency can become worthless.

On August 15, 1971, President Richard Nixon announced that the US would no longer convert dollars into gold, effectively ending the Bretton Woods system. Contrary to expectations, the dollar's value did not collapse. This stability was largely secured by a 1974 agreement with Saudi Arabia, whereby the kingdom would price its oil exclusively in U.S. dollars in exchange for American military and political support—a deal known as the petrodollar system. Because nearly every country needed to buy oil, they were compelled to hold large dollar reserves. This created sustained global demand for the dollar, allowing the U.S. to run larger trade deficits and print currency with significant flexibility. Many other countries also pegged their currencies to the dollar to ensure stability.

This system, which made the U.S. dollar the world's primary reserve currency, can be seen as a foundational element of modern global economics. Some argue it has also created imbalances that allow powerful nations to export the consequences of their monetary policies to others.

Characteristic of Money

Economists generally agree on a set of key characteristics that define sound money. To illustrate these, we will use gold as an example, a substance that has proven its ability to maintain value for thousands of years. As the world moves towards both centralized digital currencies and decentralized cryptocurrencies, understanding these foundational traits is essential. The differences between these new forms of money will be explained later.

Below is a description of the essential characteristics of money.

1. A medium of exchange

1. Money acts as a medium of exchange, enabling

transactions between individuals and businesses. It serves as an intermediary, eliminating the need for a direct barter system. For example, to trade a house for a car, you no longer need to find someone who wants your house and has the exact car you desire. Instead, you can sell your house for money and then use that money to buy a car from any dealer.

2. A unit of account

Money serves as a unit of account by providing a standard measure for valuing goods, services, assets, and debts. Prices, wages, and financial records are all expressed in this standard unit, allowing for easy comparison between completely different items.

3. Portability

Portability refers to the ease with which money can be carried and transferred. Good money should be easy to transport from one location to another without a loss of value or high transaction costs.

4. Durability

Durability is the ability of money to withstand physical wear and tear over time without degrading or losing its function. A durable form of money remains usable in the future.

5. Divisibility

Divisibility is the capability of money to be divided

into smaller units without losing its proportional value. This ensures that transactions of all sizes can be conducted accurately. For instance, a kilogram of gold can be divided into grams or ounces for smaller purchases.

6. Fungibility

Fungibility means that each unit of money is interchangeable and equal in value to another unit of the same denomination. One ounce of pure gold is identical in value to any other ounce of pure gold.

7. Limited Supply

A limited supply is crucial for money to retain its value. Gold embodies this principle; its supply is constrained by the difficulty and cost of mining and refining it. This contrasts with fiat currency, which can be created in unlimited quantities.

> **Note:**
> While a significant amount of gold is mined annually, this does not drastically devalue the metal due to the high cost and effort of production. If the market price falls below the cost of production, mining becomes unprofitable and slows down, naturally supporting price stability.

8. A store of value

A store of value is something that can be saved and retrieved in the future without significant loss of purchasing power. Gold has served this role for millennia. In contrast, the value of fiat currency is based on trust in the issuing government and can be eroded by inflation.

9. A decentralized nature

Ideal money should not be controlled by a small, privileged group. Gold is inherently decentralized; any country, business, or individual can mine and own it. National fiat currencies, however, are centrally controlled and issued by a select few. History shows that this centralized control has often led to systemic failures.

Next, we will explore how blockchain technology offers a modern solution to this problem of centralization.

Digital Currency vs Crypto Currency

The following statement will remind you if you are sometimes confused between digital and cryptocurrency without realizing the difference.

Digital currency is often centralized and controlled by a

select few, acting as a control tool. Meanwhile, cryptocurrency operates on a decentralized platform known as blockchain, designed to liberate the masses from the influence of the privileged few.

Both digital currencies and cryptocurrencies share the following characteristics of money.

Characteristic	Digital or Crypto Bitcoin?
Medium of exchange	Both
Unit of account	Both
Portability	Both
Durability	Both
Divisibility	Both
Fungibility	Both
Intrinsic value	None of them.
Limited supply	Bitcoin has a limited supply of 21 million, while the digital currency issuer can create an unlimited amount quickly, almost costlessly, and from nothing.
Decentralized	Bitcoin is decentralized, while all national digital currencies are centralized.

Digital currency worsens the issues discussed in paper currency, such as inflation, while granting governments more authority and limiting citizens' privacy and freedom. Paper currency has long been sensitive to inflation, resulting in many currencies' devaluation and eventual worthlessness throughout history, including the present time.

Authorities have often mishandled the power to control cash. Given this track record, it raises concerns about why they would seek even more power by switching to digital currency, which naturally grants them greater control.

The Power to Control Digital Currency

1. Inflation

> We have already discussed inflation and that authorities have the exclusive right to print currency without competition. Still, it is also a product that costs almost nothing to produce. Using digital cash increases authorities' power because printing and transferring money costs little, while digital cash has even fewer costs for making it out of nothing.

2. Loosing Privacy Rights

> Digital currency transactions could be subject to extensive surveillance by authorities, potentially compromising user privacy. Citizens can have some control over their money if they use cash. That is every individual's right to privacy when spending their money. You might have heard the slogan:

If you have nothing to hide, you have nothing to fear.

The previous statement is designed for mind control, which everyone must understand. The ruling class originates it—preconditions to accept something you don't need to. So, you are doing something wrong unless you grant the government access to all your spending and privacy.

The statement is designed psychologically based on "Either or," which makes most people not even think about it but react, "I have done nothing wrong and have nothing to hide, so please control all my transactions."

Why would the ruling class be exclusively granted to know everything about the people? The answer is the following slogan.

If the ruling class has nothing to hide, they have nothing to fear from the people. Therefore, the people should know where their billions came from.

That is a better slogan because the taxpayer pays them, and they own too much compared to those who pay them.

3. Block Access of Specific Individuals

Digital currency grants the ruling class the exclusive power to block people from the financial system if they do not act according to their wishes. Protesting and talking about the corruption of the government becomes automatically prohibited. That is a step toward a totalitarian regime, and all these steps are necessary to have a bit of freedom and not grant it to the authority, which already has too much power.

4. No Internet Access

What happens if you travel to a country or place without internet access, your mobile doesn't work, or you encounter any other technical issues?

5. Dependence on Technology

The widespread adoption of a digital dollar would rely heavily on digital infrastructure, potentially excluding those who need access to reliable internet or digital devices.

Characteristics of Digital Currency

Let's compare money, fiat paper currency, fiat digital currency, and cryptocurrency. We use the following as examples of the previous forms of payment systems: gold, paper dollar, digital dollar, and Bitcoin(cryptocurrency)

Gold

It is a medium of exchange, a unit of account, portable, durable, divisible, and fungible, and it has been used for thousands of years. It is also a store of value because it is used in different industries and as jewels.

Gold is in limited supply, and although many countries mine tons of gold annually, producing it is not costless. Many companies work to find, mine, and refine gold. If the price is below the effort required to make it, companies stop or reduce their time and energy expenses on gold production.

Weakness

- Gold is difficult to use for big transactions because transporting a huge amount of gold requires much effort.

Fiat paper dollar

It functions as a medium of exchange, a unit of account, and is portable, durable, divisible, and fungible.

Weakness

- As for portability, it is challenging to carry for big transactions and not easy to transfer in huge amounts, just like gold.
- Dollars don't have intrinsic value; their value decreases due to inflation and low-cost creation. In 1968, an ounce of gold was almost $35. In 2024, it becomes more than $2000.
- Its issuance and management are centralized, controlled by a select group of officials and bankers rather than being decentralized.

Fiat Digital Dollar

It is a medium of exchange, a unit of account, portable, durable, divisible, and fungible.

Weakness

- It has zero intrinsic value, and its value decreases because it can be created in large quantities at a very low cost.
- It has unlimited supply and can be almost created costlessly.
- It is a completely controlled tool by its issuers because they can track everyone's transactions and ban anyone who becomes undesirable to the ruling class.

Bitcoin

It is a medium of exchange, a unit of account, portable, durable, divisible, and fungible. Creating it is not costless or limitless because the total number of bitcoins is limited to 21 million. Producing it takes energy and time.

Bitcoin is decentralized, contrary to fiat paper currency and digital currencies such as dollars and euros. A tiny group of people cannot gain control over Bitcoin. You can transact any amount of Bitcoin directly to anyone in the world without needing a mediator or a bank. Authorities can not make excuses to confiscate it or block your account.

Weakness

- It has zero intrinsic value.
- If you lose your private key, your money is gone. Keeping Bitcoin safe is entirely the individual's responsibility. The following chapters cover several ways to keep it secure.

The Issue of Centralization

The fundamental injustice of centralized power is that it grants a small group the privilege to monitor everyone without being monitored themselves. This one-sided surveillance is inherently corrupt and has been a historical tool for control and exploitation.

The core principle of decentralization is to end this asymmetry. **No group should ever be granted the power to track the entire population without being subject to the same level of transparency.** A fair system ensures that power is accountable. This means that in a decentralized framework, surveillance is either impossible for everyone, or the "watchmen" themselves are watched by all.

3. Investing in Blockchain

In earlier chapters, fundamental concepts were introduced to emphasize the necessity of blockchain technology.

> Necessity is the mother of invention.
> *Plato*

This idea is particularly relevant because the cartel had too much power to exploit the stock markets, banks, media, and other financial and economic sectors.

People had no choice because there was no way to keep digital currencies in their digital wallets without the necessity of a bank at that time. That was also why Bitcoin gained such popularity. So many people started to post videos and messages, make documentaries, and express their support for the invention of Bitcoin, which is based on blockchain technology. The question arises: What is Bitcoin?

> Bitcoin is a decentralized online digital payment system that allows the buying, selling, and transaction of payments without an intermediary like a bank or other institution.

Satoshi Nakamoto, the inventor of Bitcoin, described the necessity of a payment system based on cryptographic proof rather than trust.

The Inventor of Bitcoin

Bitcoin was created by an anonymous individual or group known as Satoshi Nakamoto. On October 31, 2008, he released the Bitcoin white paper to a cryptography mailing list. This technical document described Bitcoin as a Peer-to-Peer Electronic Cash System and explained the specific issues it aimed to solve. Despite the widespread interest in Bitcoin's development and influence, Satoshi Nakamoto's true identity remains unrevealed.

Nakamoto mentioned that the coding work on Bitcoin started in the second quarter of 2007, and the domain name bitcoin.org was registered on August 18, 2008. On January 9, 2009, Nakamoto made the Bitcoin software publicly available on SourceForge.

He continued collaborating with other developers on the Bitcoin software until around mid-2010. According to various sources, he or they owns nearly one million Bitcoins.

Based on the available information, Satoshi Nakamoto communicated primarily through email and online forums, such as the cryptography mailing list where the Bitcoin white paper was published. There is no evidence to suggest that Nakamoto had physical contact with other programmers or individuals involved in the early development of Bitcoin. Nakamoto's identity remains a mystery, as his true identity has never been revealed.

As the story of Bitcoin and blockchain technology unfolded, it raised many critical questions. The following points analyze the forces that could be behind this creation.

- **Was Satoshi Nakamoto a government agent?**

  This question is crucial for establishing trust in Bitcoin's origins. The most logical answer is no. The core ideas of Bitcoin—decentralization, transparency, and removing financial intermediaries—directly challenge the control held by governments and central banks. It is highly unlikely that any state intelligence service would create and release a tool designed to dismantle its own monetary authority and awaken public scrutiny of the very system it controls.

- **Can we trust Bitcoin's code?**

  Bitcoin's source code is open for anyone in the world to inspect, critique, and improve. While not everyone is a programmer, a global community of expert developers continuously audits the code. This transparency creates a powerful system of checks and balances; any malicious backdoor or fundamental flaw would be rapidly exposed and impossible to conceal.

- **Why did Satoshi Nakamoto remain anonymous?**

  The most compelling reason is self-preservation. By

creating a system that disempowers central banks and governments, Satoshi made powerful enemies. Anonymity was a necessary shield against potential arrest, legal persecution, or even physical danger, ensuring that the Bitcoin project could survive and evolve without its creator becoming a target.

- **The Blockchain Doesn't Need Its Creator**

A core strength of the blockchain is that it operates independently of its creator. This can be compared to a foundational scientific theory, like those of Einstein. The theory stands on its own merits and remains valid long after its proposer is gone. If future discoveries reveal limitations in the theory, we do not accuse the original scientist of manipulation; we recognize the limits of the knowledge available at the time and build upon their work.

Similarly, Satoshi Nakamoto released this creation to the world and then stepped away. The responsibility for its continued evolution, including addressing any potential weaknesses discovered in the future, now lies with the global public and the developer community that maintains it.

Should You Invest in Bitcoin?

> **Notice**
> This book does not provide financial advice; it is solely intended for informational purposes.

An investing mindset and collected investment knowledge are two essential components for successful investing. While this book focuses on blockchain and Bitcoin investment, the principles discussed apply to other investments. Without these foundational principles, achieving success in investing would be challenging.

Some may regret not investing in cryptocurrencies early on, perceiving it as a missed opportunity. However, it's important to understand that blockchain and Bitcoin investment opportunities are not fixed moments but rather a continuous journey. For those with the right mindset, these opportunities persist, even if one seems to have been missed.

Contrary to popular belief, those who invested in Bitcoin during its early stages didn't just struggle upon significant gains; it was often a result of a prepared mindset and strategic decision-making.

Suppose an individual purchased one Bitcoin when its price was $5000. As the price fluctuated over time, dropping on some days and rising on others, the investor experienced anxiety. Eventually, after a year of volatile changes, he decided to sell when the price returned to $5000. While the cost of Bitcoin might soar to hundreds of thousands of dollars, only those who resist selling have the potential to make such significant gains. However, waiting for such a long period is a considerable risk.

This example illustrates how having the right mindset, characterized by patience, confidence, and a long-term perspective, can impact investment outcomes. While the individual invested in crypto at the right time, not having the right mindset affected the result of his investment.

The decision-making process reflects the mindset that allows the individual to resist psychologically through the market's uncertainties.

The purpose of that example is to illustrate that successful investors maintain a mindset that enables them to remain calm and rational during daily fluctuations in gains and losses. Many individuals invested in Bitcoin during its early stages when prices were low, but not all earned high profits due to psychological challenges surrounding price volatility.

Understanding key information is crucial before investing in cryptocurrency:

1. Cryptocurrency is an intangible digital currency, meaning anyone with access to your wallet's private key can spend your funds without your permission, as misuse can occur without evidence.
2. If you plan to buy a cryptocurrency and keep it on an

exchange, that is not a good strategy. This practice goes against the principles of Bitcoin, which aim to eliminate central authority. Inexperienced users have often remained in the habit of using traditional banking systems and have missed understanding blockchain technology. A notable example is the 2014 collapse of Mt. Gox, one of the largest Bitcoin exchanges, which resulted in the loss of hundreds of thousands of bitcoins. Limiting your use of exchanges to small amounts is advisable to avoid this risk, thereby reducing potential losses.

3. Were you aware that over thousands cryptocurrencies exist today, many designed to become obsolete eventually? So, before investing in any cryptocurrency, take time to study it.

4. Were you aware that if a cryptocurrency is not open source, investing in it will likely lead to eventual financial loss, even if short-term profits are made?

5. Storing your funds in a digital wallet on an external hard drive or paper wallet is often more secure than relying on centralized exchanges. However, this method requires knowledge to set up and secure the digital wallet effectively.

6. Did you know that some individuals owned significant amounts during Bitcoin's early days when its price was a few cents? However, as the price surged, some forgot their wallet passwords, losing many bitcoins worth millions of dollars.

7. When we talk about crypto, we know that mobile

phones or computers are mostly used for this purpose. Have you ever thought that some malware programs could be installed without your knowledge on your computer? And that you might not be alone, with eyes behind the scenes watching your steps? Some governments have a back door to access your computer's or mobile operating system. If you're unaware of that, think carefully and choose an operating system that is safe and preferable to be an open source.

Many experts at the beginning of the invention of Bitcoin in 2009, when the price was no more than a few cents of the dollar, expected that the price would increase significantly and be a very good investment for the future. That's when their predictions came true: within a decade, the Bitcoin price went from a few cents to tens of thousands of dollars.

Unveiling Bitcoin's Security Risks

When you decide to invest in Bitcoin and other cryptocurrencies, it's crucial to be mindful of potential threats, as outlined below. Certain programs can compromise the security of your Bitcoin holdings or other cryptocurrencies.

1. Malware

Diverse malicious software could be installed on your computer without your consent or other devices to monitor your activities. This type of malware can target cryptocurrency wallets and copy your digital wallets, private keys, and passwords.

2. Phishing

Phishing attackers may send fake emails or create fake websites that simulate cryptocurrency exchanges or wallets, asking users to enter their login or private keys.

3. Fake Wallet Apps

Fake wallet applications may appear legitimate but are designed to steal cryptocurrencies once you deposit funds. These apps often are offered through unofficial app stores or websites.

4. Ponzi Schemes

Some programs are designed as Ponzi schemes and use new investors' funds to pay back earlier investors rather than generate real profits.

5. Fake ICOs

Initial Coin Offerings (ICOs) collect funds for new cryptocurrency projects. Scammers can ask for funds and disappear without delivering the products or services.

6. Cryptojacking

That aims to infect computers or websites with malware to mine cryptocurrencies without the owner's consent. The target here is not directly stealing digital wallets, but it leads to financial loss through the overuse of electricity.

To protect yourself against these threats, you must keep your software up-to-date and use trusted antivirus software. Storing your cryptocurrency in hardware wallets or cold storage can provide extra protection against theft.

Private Keys and Public Keys

Private keys are used to access and spend Bitcoin funds, while public keys generate Bitcoin addresses like bank accounts to receive funds. It's important to keep private keys secure and never share them with anyone, as they provide complete control over your Bitcoin holdings.

Bitcoin Storage Methods

The following methods and tools store Bitcoin and other cryptocurrencies' holdings.

1. Personal Wallets

Software Wallets

You can install an application or software program on

computers, smartphones, or other devices. With these tools, you can create your wallet and manage transactions. It's crucial to back up the wallet on an external device and avoid leaving it on a computer connected to the internet to ensure the security of your wallet,

Hardware Wallets

Several hardware or physical devices are designed to store cryptocurrency private keys offline, providing high security.

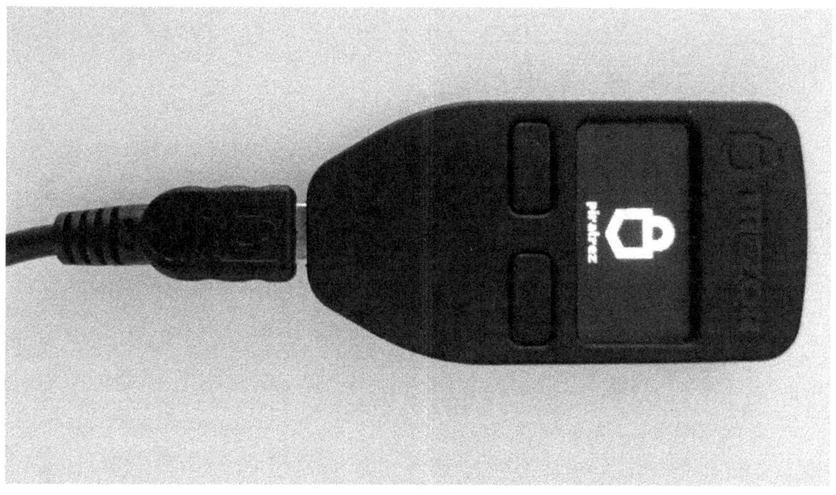

Paper Wallets

These paper wallets are physical copies or printouts of Bitcoin public and private keys, often generated offline for added security. They are recommended because they store your Bitcoin funds offline. A paper wallet contains a private key, so it should be kept secure and out of reach.

2. Exchange Wallets

Cryptocurrency exchanges provide wallets for storing Bitcoin purchased or traded on their platforms. These types of wallets are not recommended for storing large amounts because you risk losing your funds if the exchange is hacked or bankrupted. They use a third-party service similar to the current banking system.

The choice of a wallet depends on security and convenience. Personal offline wallets, such as paper and hardware wallets, are preferred for large amounts of money. Exchange wallets are convenient for small amounts of money and easy transactions.

Professionals vs Beginner Investors

While some investors have earned fortunes by wisely investing in Bitcoin, cryptocurrencies, and blockchain applications, many others regret not discovering these technologies sooner or failing to seize the opportunity. The reality is that successful investors ensure they engage with investments strategically and with understanding.
It's important to note that the price of Bitcoin changes continuously, often dropping by several thousand dollars one day and then surging by the same amount the next. Beginner investors tend to purchase when prices rise and sell in a panic when they observe a decline. In contrast, experienced investors often adopt a contrary approach, buying during price drops and strategically selling during rallies. This patient, disciplined approach is a key to successful investment.

It's also crucial to recognize that when the price of Bitcoin increases substantially relative to the dollar, it doesn't necessarily imply a precise rise in its intrinsic value. A critical part of this analysis is considering the unstable and often declining value of the dollar and other fiat currencies due to inflation.

Inexperienced investors often expect rapid wealth accumulation. However, seasoned investors understand the risks. They diversify their investments across multiple assets, a strategy that not only minimizes the risk of catastrophic loss but also provides a sense of security and confidence

The Psychology of Investments

Investing is a complex psychological effort, particularly challenging when faced with volatile price swings. As prices soar, the urge to sell can become overwhelming. Rumors spread, suggesting that Bitcoin and blockchain technology are on the brink of failure or that upcoming government regulations will make investments worthless. Faced with such uncertainty, many rush to sell before potential losses. However, while prices may skyrocket or plummet, future prices remain uncertain. Bitcoin's value could reach ultimate heights or be reduced to nothing. The key lies in maintaining an organized mindset amid significant price fluctuations. By doing so, you could seize opportunities others might miss, leading to substantial gains in your investments.

Diversifying across various assets is an effective strategy for withstanding the psychological pressures of investing. Cryptocurrencies, real estate, precious metals, diamonds, gemstones, energy, stock markets, and rare collectibles like watches and paintings are other alternative investments that offer a barrier against market volatility.

Yet, it's critical to approach diversification effectively, as investing in unfamiliar assets without sufficient knowledge can be highly risky.

In essence, successful investing demands discipline and a dedicated mindset. Investors can more effectively navigate the market's stormy gulfs by resisting impulsive reactions to price movements and embracing diversification with informed decision-making.

4. Blockchain Types

As previously explained, blockchain technology offers an alternative to the centralized system based on trusting a tiny group of people with power over the majority.
However, a potential concern arises as the authority may not embrace this system, instead seeking to exercise further control by implementing completely centralized digital currencies. By applying digital fiat currency, the authority gains even more power to suggest more rules and regulations.

Types of Consensus Mechanism

Different consensus mechanisms are used in blockchain networks. The most common are Proof of Work (PoW) and Proof of Stake (PoS).

Proof of work (PoW)

In PoW, miners compete to solve mathematical puzzles to validate transactions. The first to solve the puzzle adds a new block to the blockchain and receives a reward in Bitcoin.

Proof of Stake (Pos)

In PoS, miners are chosen to validate transactions randomly,

but their chance of being selected is also based on the amount of cryptocurrency they hold and are willing to stake (lock up). The PoS mining mechanism consumes less energy than PoW.
Examples of proof of stake are Cardano and Ethereum 2.0.

Types of Blockchain

There are several types of blockchains, each with its applications and usages. The two main categories are public and private blockchains, but more types are explained below.

It's crucial to note that while banks and governments may utilize blockchain technology for practical purposes, their implementations often differ from the decentralized and transparent models. Instead, they may be used for centralized, controlled blockchains.

1. Public Blockchains

This type of blockchain is permissionless and open for anyone to use, add blocks to, or mine if they have the necessary tools, software, and devices. It doesn't require participation permission; everyone can download the entire blockchain and transaction history. Thus, it is transparent and decentralized, and no single entity controls the network. An example of a public blockchain is Bitcoin. Anyone with an internet connection can access the public blockchain.

Advantages

1. Decentralization
Decentralized networks have no single entity in charge and no single point of attack. As a democratic system, no censorship is possible.

2. Transparency

The public blockchain is transparent, and all transactions are visible. Therefore, no trust is required, and no one needs to be held accountable.

3. Security

The technology does not allow data to be edited on the blockchain without the agreement of the other participants. Once a transaction is approved, it is secured by a cryptographic mechanism.

4. Accessibility

A public blockchain is accessible to anyone with internet access.

5. Open Source

A public blockchain is often programmed with open-source code available for anyone to check how it works.

6. Limited Supply

The advantage of using this type of blockchain for payment systems such as Bitcoin is that the maximum number of bitcoins that can be created is known as 21 million. This limited number completely differs from fiat currency, which has an unlimited supply.

Disadvantages

1. Scalability
Public blockchain can face scalability issues due to worldwide usage and extreme transactions.

2. Energy consumption

Bitcoin is based on proof-of-work (PoW) consensus mechanisms. Therefore, maintaining the network's life consumes a lot of energy.

3. Although people can transact using different wallet addresses, Bitcoin is not completely private. However, some types of cryptocurrencies offer more privacy.

Practical Implementations

Public blockchain can be used for voting systems to improve trust and transparency, smart contracts, supply chain management, intellectual property protection, and more.

2. Private Blockchains

This type of blockchain is restricted to only those with

permission to participate. It is centralized, and a single entity, organization, or group controls it. The data can also be seen only by those who can access it.

Advantages

1. Privacy

Private blockchains offer privacy and restricted access to the data to only authorized participants.

2. Better Scalability

With significantly fewer participants than public blockchains, this type of blockchain operates at a remarkable speed, showcasing its efficiency.

3. More control

A few members of an organization control this type of blockchain. That could have an advantage for the organization, but it differs from the public blockchain.

4. Reduced energy consumption

Privat blockchains typically use consensus mechanisms that require less energy compared to proof-of-work.

Practical Implementations

1. Managing the supply chain.
2. Track and verify asset ownership.

3. Internal voting.

Disadvantages

1. Centralization
Private blockchain is centralized and controlled by a single entity, which is risky because it has a single point of failure.

2. Reduced Transparency
It is not transparent and is based on trust.

3. Hybrid Blockchain

Hybrid blockchain technology enables businesses to establish a dual system that includes private, permission-based elements and public, permissionless components. This approach grants organizations control over data access, allowing them to regulate which parties can access specific data stored on the blockchain while determining the information available to the public.

Advantages

1. Security
The private part is closed to the public; therefore, an outsider cannot launch a 51 attack on the network.
2. Speed
The participants of this blockchain are limited; therefore, the network is faster than the public blockchain.

Disadvantages

1. Not Transparent

While the system is not completely transparent, it ensures controlled access to the private part, which is only accessible to certain members, providing a clear understanding of who has access to what.

2. Centralization

The network is partly centralized.

Practical Implementations

This type of blockchain is practical for use in real estate and provides the public with the information they need.

4. Consortium (Federated) Blockchain

A consortium blockchain is similar to a hybrid because it uses private and public components. This type allows organizations to share blockchain data to reach a decentralized consensus.

Advantages

It is secure and faster compared to the public blockchain.

Disadvantages

It is not completely transparent, and it has private access.

Practical Implementations

1. Banks Implementation

A group of banks can use consortium blockchain to share data transactions that allow customers of one bank to use the service of the other banks. That facilitates their services for their customers.

2. Food Tracking

The food process starts with the farmers, is delivered to the central place, and then distributed over the supermarkets. Those organizations can use a consortium blockchain to reach a consensus in a decentralized manner.

5. Blockchain Supports Mind Freedom

Controlling the creation of money grants a small group immense influence, which often extends to acquiring major media outlets and news channels with large audiences.

For any powerful group, managing the flow of information is a primary concern. There is a strong incentive to influence the major platforms where public discourse happens. When a single entity owns a media or social media platform, it can lead to the silencing of voices and stories that challenge the prevailing narrative.

In many ways, an uncontrolled truth is the greatest challenge to any entrenched power structure.

The result can be a dominant narrative that aligns with a specific agenda. We've seen various social media platforms ban certain individuals for years, citing violations of guidelines or the spread of misinformation. This pattern raises a critical question: are these platforms truly independent competitors, or is there a level of coordination or shared interest among them? Furthermore, could the same influential groups hold significant, undisclosed stakes across multiple media companies?

The long-standing use of narrative control is particularly concerning because its mechanisms are often invisible to the public.

Blockchain technology has the potential to challenge this model of information control by enabling a freer and more transparent flow of information. Promisingly, new social media platforms and search engines are already being built on this technology, offering a foundation for a more democratic digital space.

While we often hear about propaganda used by media and politicians, the most crucial step is for individuals to cultivate a habit of looking deeper. We must actively seek to understand how influence works.

Since most mainstream media is centralized—much like the currency system—it highlights why powerful groups have a strong interest in controlling these channels and limiting exposure to alternative news sources.

But first, it's essential to understand the power of the subconscious mind and the techniques used to influence it. To see how public perception is shaped on a daily basis to align with a system, we must explore how media can be used to guide mass thought patterns.

The Subconscious Mind Power

You have likely heard that we all possess more power than we realize. Let's clarify this with concrete examples. Have you ever wondered why learning to swim, speak a foreign language, ride a bicycle, drive a car, play an instrument, or speak in public requires so much repetition? Once you master these skills through practice, you can perform them automatically, without conscious effort or nervousness.

What Is the Subconscious Mind?

The "subconscious" is the part of your mind that operates below your active awareness. It is a vast storehouse of information, memories, habits, beliefs, and skills that you are not constantly thinking about but can access when needed. Everything you learn is stored in the subconscious like a database. It is an incredibly powerful force, accounting for almost 90% of your mental activity and profoundly influencing your daily life.

The first step to harnessing this power is to learn how to reprogram it to change habits or achieve new outcomes. Methods for this include affirmations, visualization, hypnosis, subliminal messages, and consistent practice. But before you begin reprogramming, it is essential to understand how the subconscious mind operates.

Recall how, when you first learned to drive, you had to concentrate intensely on every technical detail. As your subconscious mind gradually absorbed the skill, driving became an automatic and effortless task. Mastering this new skill freed your conscious mind, allowing you to hold conversations and focus on the road ahead without fatigue.

How the Subconscious Mind Works?

1. **It Accepts Information by Repetition, Not Logic:** Unlike the conscious mind, the subconscious operates non-critically, adopting beliefs through repeated exposure rather than evidence or logic. This principle has been used throughout history to influence public opinion. Politicians and media often use propaganda to shape beliefs, a famous example being the Nazi propaganda machine.

   "If you tell a big enough lie and tell it frequently enough, it will be believed."

2. **It Blurs Reality and Imagination:** The subconscious mind can trigger physical reactions based on vivid imagination. For example, picturing yourself jumping into the ocean can increase your heart rate, even though you consciously know you are safe.

3. **It Understands Only the Present Tense:** The subconscious processes information in the "now." To reprogram it effectively, use present-tense affirmations like "I am happy" or "I have a fulfilling career," rather than future or past statements like "I

will be happy" or "I was successful."

4. **It Learns Through Repetition:** Consistent repetition is key to embedding new beliefs. The subconscious learns by repeatedly visualizing a goal or rehearsing a new behavior.

5. **It Responds to Emotion:** For an idea to take root, it must be paired with strong, positive emotions. Merely repeating "I am prosperous" is less effective than truly feeling the joy and security of being prosperous.

6. **It Processes Positive Language:** The subconscious struggles with negation. A statement like "I am not overweight" is interpreted with a focus on "overweight." Instead, use positive affirmations like "I am fit and healthy" to direct focus toward the desired outcome.

7. **It Thinks in Abstract Concepts, Not Numbers:** When reprogramming for wealth, focus on the feeling of "abundance" or "financial freedom" rather than a specific numerical target, as the subconscious understands concepts better than figures.

8. **It Manages Automatic Bodily Functions:** It controls essential processes like breathing, heartbeat, and digestion automatically, even while you sleep.

9. **It is Always Active:** The subconscious mind never

sleeps; it remains active 24 hours a day.

10. **Its Primary Goal is Survival:** Its fundamental drive is to keep you safe and alive, which can sometimes override goals for happiness or success if they are perceived as threats.

Adevertising and Mind Programming

Have you ever noticed how companies consistently place their logos in football stadiums, on tennis players' shirts, or during international events? Often, they aren't promoting a specific product, but using repetition to make their brand familiar to our subconscious.

Through repeated exposure, these logos become associated with quality and success, especially when linked to popular teams or celebrities. This is why you might instinctively perceive these brands as premium when you see them in stores—the significant investment in advertising is often reflected in the product's price.

This form of branding is highly effective and will continue as long as it drives profits. It's not a critique of marketing itself, but it's worth noting that extensive advertising campaigns can influence product pricing, sometimes making it less about the item's inherent quality and more about the brand perception they've built.

Accessing Your Subconscious Mind

Our subconscious minds are shaped from a very young age, long before we can consciously choose what to believe. Our families, schools, communities, and the media all contribute to this early programming. While this foundation is essential, not all the beliefs we inherit serve our adult goals; some can be limiting or irrational.

For example, children often adopt their family's religious or cultural views without question. While these beliefs provide a vital sense of identity and belonging, some may later conflict with personal aspirations. The good news is that we can reassess these deeply held beliefs. By consciously updating our internal programming, we can remove mental barriers and make our path to success smoother and more direct.

Think of skills like riding a bike or speaking a language—once learned, they are difficult to unlearn. This shows how durable subconscious programming can be. This is also why it's so powerful to install positive and empowering beliefs from the start, saving the considerable effort needed to change them later.

This durability of early learning is also why many forms of influence, including advertising and civic education, often focus on children. Young minds are naturally open and receptive, forming the core beliefs that will guide them throughout their lives.

Habits and the Subconscious Mind

Some of the habits we form can unintentionally create challenges in our lives, acting as quiet barriers that can hold us back from reaching our full potential.
This is why learning to identify and gently reshape these unconscious patterns is so important. For example, if someone habitually feels resentment toward financial success, they may unknowingly be reinforcing a mindset of limitation. These repeated thoughts and emotions don't affect the wealthy but can create an internal glass ceiling for the person holding them.

This is the same principle behind positive affirmations and visualization. Our subconscious mind learns through repetition. By consistently focusing on thoughts of lack, we can unintentionally train ourselves to stay in a cycle of struggle. Often, when a goal feels out of reach, it's because our conscious desire hasn't yet been aligned with our deeper subconscious beliefs.

The exciting part is that we can reprogram these patterns. By consciously feeding our subconscious mind with beliefs of abundance and success, we can replace self-limiting habits and naturally move toward the outcomes we truly desire.

Cultural and Religious Beliefs

The subconscious mind helps explain why different cultures hold such varied beliefs. For instance, in Western cultures, dogs are often beloved pets. In some Eastern cultures, they may be viewed as a food source, while in parts of the Middle East, they are traditionally considered unclean.

If you were to ask someone from any of these backgrounds which view is "correct," they would likely instinctively defend their own culture's perspective. This demonstrates how our deeply ingrained subconscious beliefs often hold more immediate sway than our conscious, rational thoughts.

This shows the profound power of the subconscious. Once a belief is set, changing it requires conscious effort. Imagine being raised to believe that wealthy people are inherently bad. If you then desire wealth, your own subconscious mind could be working against your goal without you even realizing it.

We see this in relationships, too. When someone says, "All men are the same" or "All women are the same," it often points to a painful emotional pattern. To find a healthy relationship, the work often begins with gently reprogramming these underlying beliefs.

This principle of repetition is also seen in many religious practices, where followers repeat affirmations or prayers throughout their lives. This isn't because a divine power is hard of hearing, but because the repetition serves to deeply embed the beliefs within the individual's own subconscious. This creates a strong, internalized faith that guides their actions.

Ultimately, while our subconscious programming provides a sense of security, it's empowering to learn how to consciously filter and update these beliefs. This allows us to ensure our inner world is serving our own goals and well-being, rather than just echoing the influences of our past.

Protecting the Subconscious Mind

Recognizing intentional programming and filtering it on a conscious level is essential for protecting your subconscious mind against unwanted influences, whether from external sources or your thoughts. By recognizing this process, you empower your conscious mind to choose incoming information before it penetrates the subconscious domain. Have you ever considered why crucial understandings like this are seldom presented within the educational system? The answer lies in the ruling class's agenda, which prioritizes obedient workers over independent thinkers.

Centralized Social Media Platforms

The information about programming the subconscious mind discussed above is frequently used by most large social media platforms to shape the mindsets of the masses. These platforms are essential for the ruling class, leading to their continual demand for new popular media organizations.

As people innocently watch the news and other programs on these platforms, fear is consistently implanted in the minds of the masses. This fear often rotates around the possibility of wars, even though many wars are initiated by the same groups who control these companies and even the arms industry.

War is considered one of the most profitable businesses for the ruling class because taxpayers pay the costs and bear the consequences while the profits flow directly to those who initiate it. The masses are continually scared by their media and programmed subconsciously to accept it.

Decentralized Blockchain Based Media

Many mistakenly believe that blockchain technology is solely intended for creating payment systems, but this couldn't be further from the truth. Blockchain technology can potentially liberate humanity in various aspects of life. Imagine a decentralized social media platform built on blockchain technology.

Imagine no one can censor messages and videos, and there's no bias in promoting certain individuals or companies and banning others. The popularity of content depends solely on the public's desires.

The good news is that such platforms already exist. However, they still need further development as they have only gained support from those who understand the concept and potential of blockchain technology.

These platforms are yet to gain widespread popularity. With blockchain technology, you can create decentralized search engines, social media platforms, and much more, effectively ending the control of the few and their manipulation of minds and perceptions.

What Is Mindset?

A mindset is a collection of beliefs, habits, principles, and cultural influences that guide an individual. It sets perspectives, directs actions, and ultimately shapes one's life. The outcomes one achieves are directly tied to this internal framework. These deeply held beliefs largely dictate our choices and behaviors.

This is because a mindset is primarily formed through subconscious programming over a lifetime. While this programming significantly guides an individual, it's crucial to recognize that these patterns can be identified and reshaped.

Altering Your Mindset

Understanding the process of altering mindset is crucial for empowering individuals to navigate their thoughts and beliefs effectively. Most people's priorities often revolve around quick wealth accumulation and achieving desires quickly without understanding the basic and necessary knowledge to accomplish them.
A simple online search reveals an overload of resources promising quick accomplishes for various goals, from wealth accumulation to language mastery. However, a deeper exploration of mindset alteration can unveil a more sustainable path to personal development.

 Any goals you want to achieve without developing the mindset to be aligned with those goals results in struggle.

Mindset Is Invisible

It is challenging to understand the effectiveness of mindset because it operates invisibly to the outside observer. The only mindset visible is the one we possess. The complexity arises from attempting to evaluate the mind using the mind itself. However, nearly everyone's mindset can be concluded from their actions, as mindset influences behavior, and behavior causes observable outcomes.
Consider a religious mindset, which often leads individuals to gather in places of worship to connect with like-minded people. Similarly, a mindset focused on success might

prompt actions such as networking with companies or researching public demand. A scientific mindset might lead to engagement with communities of fellow scientists. Even a health-oriented mindset can be seen in actions like participating in sports, studying healthy food, and adopting specific diets. Each of these actions is a direct result of the mindset guiding them.

Remarkably, the mind can be focused on multiple objectives simultaneously. Ultimately, mindset shapes actions, and actions determine outcomes.

6. The Wisdom of Open Mind

The misconception surrounding blockchain often reduces it to being solely a solution for financial systems, failing to recognize its vast implications across numerous aspects of our lives, including philosophical ideas. Blockchain technology extends far beyond finance, involving almost every aspect of our existence, shaping how we perform transactions, and influencing our intellectual understanding of trust, transparency, and decentralization.

Imagine a world where you are born into a country whose rules and values don't align with yours. Despite this, you must accept its regulations simply because of your birthplace. However, with the birth of blockchain technology, living in the country of your choice and contributing taxes to a government whose principles resonate with yours becomes a feasible reality.

The concept of decentralization encourages healthy competition among nations rather than solely competing to enrich and empower the elite. Countries would strive to provide optimal conditions for their citizens, creating a circumstance where the people's interests take priority over the interests of a select few.

The longer you live and learn, the more you discover the necessity of an open mind. In a world where everything, including scientific theories, is subject to change, sticking to static beliefs can lead to stagnation and struggle.

Questioning and Adapting New Ideas

This chapter highlights the vision that nothing is impossible and that knowledge always evolves. Embracing this concept can illuminate the wisdom of questioning established beliefs and remaining open to new ideas.

The following knowledge clarifies the importance of questioning traditional wisdom.
Traditional values and religious beliefs are often implanted in an individual's mind from childhood, regardless of their integrity. Diverse nations hold their cultural ideas. Contrarily, there's widespread agreement regarding science that it represents the ultimate truth, given its universal application and development across countries.

However, the concept that science represents the ultimate truth is not accurate. Scientific knowledge evolves and is subject to updates. Therefore, while science offers valuable understandings and practical applications, it remains to be questioned whether it provides the ultimate truth. The answer is, let's study it and challenge it.

Imagination or Science?

Someone published a theory that suggests time is not constant as we know it for ages. According to that theory, a father could end up younger than his child. Consider this scenario: a father, aged 20, has a two-year-old child.

Now, let's imagine that this person travels through space for 15 years at 90 percent of the speed of light. Upon returning to Earth, he will have aged 35. However, astonishingly, his child will have aged to 37. This difference arises because the 15 years spent in space, from the father's perspective, equals 35 years passing on Earth.

Is this idea simply an imagination? Not at all. This theory was developed by none other than Albert Einstein. Initially met with skepticism, it caused a scientific revolution. Yet, over time, it was proven that the faster the speed, the slower time passes.

To illustrate this concept, I have written a simple computer program to calculate the father's age after the space journey and the time that passes during the trip.

If you are familiar with Python, you can install it and run the following program. You can input different ages for the father and child and the number of years passed on Earth. The program will then calculate the travel time in years and the father's age.

Below are the specific details to input into the program:

Initial Father's age: 20 years
Initial Child's age: 2 years
Years passed on Earth: 35 years
Speed of the spacecraft: 90% of the speed of light

> **Notice**
>
> The speed of light is considered 100% and equal to 3 x 10 ^ 8 m/s.

The program will then calculate the following:

1. Travel time
2. The age of the father after the journey.

```python
import math

# Choose "years" as the unit of time.
age_father = int(input("Enter the age of the father: "))
age_child = int(input("Enter the age of the child: "))

# Enter the number of years passed on Earth.
time_on_earth = int(input("Enter the years passed on
Earth: "))


c = 10 * (3 ** 8)   # The speed of light.
# Enter the spacecraft speed as a percentage of the
speed of light.
velocity_spacecraft = int(input("Enter the spacecraft
speed (percentage): "))
velocity_spacecraft = (velocity_spacecraft/100) * c
# Use the formula of the time dilation equation.
```

```python
travel_time = time_on_earth * math.sqrt(1 -
(velocity_spacecraft ** 2) / (c ** 2))

age_father_after = age_father + travel_time
age_child_after = age_child + time_on_earth

print(".....................")
print("Time passed during travel: %.1f" % travel_time,
"years")
print("Age of the father: %.1f" % age_father_after,
"years")
print("Age of the child : ", age_child_after, "years\n")
```

The output of the program

```
Enter the age of the father: 20
Enter the age of the child: 2
Enter the years passed on Earth: 35
Enter the spacecraft speed (percentage): 90

.....................
Time passed during travel: 15.3 years
Age of the father: 35.3 years
Age of the child :  37 years
```

We'll use all the previous information, with the only change being the increase in the spacecraft's speed to 99 percent of the speed of light. Upon running the program, the output reveals that the father's age is almost 25 this time, whereas his child's age on Earth remains 37.

That means the increase in the spacecraft's speed keeps the father even younger, and the age difference between him and his child becomes almost 12 years.

This example demonstrates the power of questioning beliefs. For thousands of years, we believed that time was an immutable constant. Yet, the discovery of time dilation destroyed this concept, pushing us into a new era of understanding the universe.

The output based on the speed of 99%

```
Enter the age of the father: 20
Enter the age of the child: 2
Enter the years passed on Earth: 35
Enter the spacecraft speed (percentage): 99
.....................
Time passed during travel: 4.9 years
Age of the father: 24.9 years
Age of the child :  37 years
```

Some concepts of the theory of relativity have surprised many as they challenge our classical conceptions of time and space, which were previously thought fixed. The relativity theory is not science fiction; precise experiments have proven it.

Speed of Light

When you turn on a light switch, the space is instantly illuminated. This rapid illumination shows that light travels at a very high speed, nearly 3 x 10^8 meters per second. This constant speed of light is represented by the symbol "c." According to the relativity, nothing in the universe can surpass the speed of light.

This theory was a game-changer, explaining why some of Isaac Newton's laws in physics fail to apply to objects moving at high speeds. According to Einstein, if one could travel at the speed of light, time would effectively stop, leading to eternal existence. In a mind-boggling theoretical scenario where traveling faster than the speed of light is possible, one might even travel backward in time. The previous example of the father and his child showed that the father stays younger by increasing the spacecraft's speed.

Length Contraction

The length of a moving object is contracted in the direction of its motion. We can accurately calculate this phenomenon using the following mathematical formula. As an object moves faster, it becomes shorter. This effect becomes increasingly noticeable as the object's speed approaches the speed of light.

For instance, if an object travels at 0.99 times the speed of light, its length decreases from 20 m to almost 3 m. The following Python program demonstrates how to calculate this length using the contraction equation.

```python
import math


L0 = 20 # 20 meters object length on earth
c = 3 * (10 ** 8) # m/s speed of light
velocity_spacecraft = 0.99 * c
# the length of the object wihin the spacecraft in the
```

```
direction of motion
L= L0 * math.sqrt(1-(velocity_spacecraft **2 /c ** 2))

print("The length of the object becomes: %.1f" % L,
"meters")
```

The length of the object becomes: 2.8 meters

Humanity assumed that the length of a foot or a meter remained constant for millennia under all circumstances. However, new phenomena fundamentally challenge this longstanding belief. As time progresses, it becomes increasingly evident that we must remain open to new ideas and paradigms.

I won't delve too deeply into the domain of science, but numerous quantum phenomena also challenge centuries-old beliefs.

Cultural Beliefs

Since birth, our minds have been shaped by intentional and unintentional programming, forming our beliefs about religion, cultural traditions, and even groundless fears. In the previous chapters, I explored the scientific principles behind this programming.

My life among diverse cultures fascinated me by how different cultures have shaped different opinions about some creatures, such as rats, mice, or spiders. For instance, while some cultures view rats with disgust, others keep them as pets, and astonishingly, some even prepare a meal from them.

Similarly, attitudes toward spiders vary greatly among different traditions. Some cultures fear them, while others are fine with them.

It's important to remember that these cultural beliefs are not objective truths but products of our individual and collective mind programming.

Arguing that any of these beliefs represent the ultimate truth would be subjective, as people can be reprogrammed to switch from one cultural belief to another and one religion to another.

Similarly, we've been conditioned to believe that there's only one way to organize society: by trusting a select few individuals to lead and make significant decisions.

Blockchain technology has the potential to change many aspects of our lives. However, governments worldwide have not embraced the idea of being relieved of their heavy responsibilities. Instead, many criticize the technology and associate it with harmful concepts.

If there are issues with the idea or the technology itself, governments have the means to invest taxpayer money to improve it. However, they often prioritize funding wars and other unpopular investments over addressing societal needs.

Taxpayers contribute to government funds, yet the government can monitor every aspect of taxpayers' spending, while citizens need access to information about where their taxes are spent. How does the government justify making decisions to allocate billions of dollars without transparency to those who provide those funds?

So far, people have generally accepted placing their trust in a few leaders. However, with the birth of tools that can replace trust with transparency, this should no longer be a problem for the ruling class.

How to recognize truth?

Discussions about truth often involve complex philosophical and scientific debates. While the nature of reality may be subject to interpretation, its purpose remains fundamental to our understanding and knowledge.

Truth is fundamentally relative and depends on factors such as time and place. For example, our current theoretical description of electrons has enabled us to build countless working technological devices. If future discoveries reveal different behaviors, it won't mean our current understanding was "false," but rather that it was a useful and necessary part of a broader, more general theory.

We can adapt this principle to human experience. Our fear of high temperatures is a truth based on our body's limited resistance. However, if we could someday withstand those temperatures, that specific fear would become groundless. The functional truth changed when the context did.

Grasping the truth is crucial for survival and a key to our evolution. The truths we hold precious today might be unimportant in the future. The knowledge that shapes one culture's identity could be utterly foreign to another.
The same applies to prehistoric humans; they feared wild animals and diseases that pose little threat to us today. This shows that even our fears are subject to evolution, which applies to almost every aspect of our lives.

Our fears are more evolved than those of prehistoric humans because we have defeated many threatening species using our intellect, and some of those animals have even gone extinct. However, we must always deal with the truth of the present moment. There is a fear that the sun might lose its energy after a few billion years, but that is only a concern for now. In the future, humans might create an artificial sun that is even better and more controllable than the natural one.

The question of what the truth is rather complicated because most people assume they know its concept without doubt.
Let's discuss the idea.
Below are some important concepts that should be

considered when recognizing the truth. Truth is a relative concept. It is not absolute and doesn't apply to all times and places. The previous examples showed that truths recognized for ages are subject to updates.

Here, we present some common approaches that can lead to recognizing truth.

1. Experiential Evidence

Truth can be recognized through scientific experimentation and observation. The proof that this concept works is visible in the technology humanity has achieved, the advanced space industry, and other areas based on scientific investigations.

2. Logic and Reasoning

Logical reasoning involves evaluating arguments based on established rules. If the premises are true and the logic is sound, the conclusion must also be true. Examples are:
* Premise 1: David is 180 cm tall.
* Premise 2: David is the same height as Jack.
* Conclusion: Therefore, Jack is 180 cm tall.
* Premise 1: All living beings are mortal.
* Premise 2: Humans are living beings.
* Conclusion: Therefore, humans are mortal.

3. Consensus and Agreement

Truth can be recognized through consensus. This can be an agreement among experts who review evidence, or a technical consensus in a decentralized, transparent system like a **blockchain**. This new method of consensus is not subject to control and manipulation by a few people, as the rules are open for anyone to verify.

Blockchain Is the Answer

Human beings are pushed to accept certain ideas and traditional cultural norms as absolute truths, often without questioning them. Across millennia, societies have chosen a select few individuals for governance. Yet, this practice remains largely unchallenged, without consideration of whether it remains the sole possible approach for societal functioning.

In the digital age, governing people can pose extreme dangers. A select few can impose their will over the majority, potentially exploiting it for personal gain. As rulers advocate for increased digital control, the emergence of blockchain technology offers a counterbalance. Blockchain has the potential to decentralize authority's power, undermine the ultimate control by providing transparency, and empower individuals with greater freedom. At the same time, it can reduce and limit the ruling class's power.

7. Democratizing AI with Blockchain

For thousands of years, humanity relied on trusting a ruling class to govern society. Unfortunately, this centralized power was often exploited, serving the interests of a few at the expense of the many. A practical solution to decentralize this power remained elusive because the necessary technology simply did not exist.

Democracy emerged as a physical attempt to decentralize governance. The idea is profound and has, to some level, succeeded in granting individuals more freedom. However, in practice, its execution often falls short. Many democratic nations are fundamentally corrupt, with leaders tending to protect their own interests rather than those of the people they serve—a potential flaw of human nature.

About twenty-five years ago, visionaries proclaimed that Artificial Intelligence (AI) would shape the future. At the time, this was difficult for many to grasp, as the internet and personal computing were still in their infancy.

Today, the significance of that prediction is becoming clear. Many still do not grasp the monumental shift AI represents. It is a revolutionary force that will push society toward one of two extremes: unprecedented individual freedom or ultimate centralized control. The outcome depends entirely on how humanity—both the people and the powerful—chooses to guide this transformation.

Artificial Intelligence Awareness

A technological shift of this magnitude forces the ruling class to decide how to maintain its control. If this new power falls into the wrong hands, it could grant them near-total authority over the population.

In our current system, a crucial limit on power exists: law enforcement is made up of human beings. Humans only obey authority to a point. If commands become too extreme or immoral, police may refuse to carry them out due to their own emotions, compassion, and moral judgment. They are vulnerable, feel fear, and can be held accountable.

With Artificial Intelligence, this dynamic changes completely. The ruling class could bypass human enforcers entirely. AI lacks fear, compassion, and a sense of morality. It does not worry about survival or accountability. This makes it the perfect tool for absolute control.

AI-controlled robots, immune to injury and deployed with heavy weapons, could be used against citizens without hesitation. We already see precursors to this with centralized drone systems that can strike targets remotely.

Now, imagine this power combined with the advanced reasoning of modern AI. Physical forms, integrated into society, could replace traditional police and armies with autonomous drones, self-driving cars, and automated security guards.

This leads to the essential question: In such a scenario, what would remain of human freedom, and how could society possibly defend itself?

The Danger of Centralized Controlled AI

In considering the evolution of governance systems, we observe that stability and oversight are often primary concerns for governing bodies. The transition toward centralized AI systems presents an opportunity to enhance administrative efficiency, but also raises important questions about the balance of power.

When AI systems become tools of governance without adequate public oversight, there is potential for concerning developments. These may include the gradual erosion of open discourse and the marginalization of dissenting perspectives. Without robust democratic safeguards, such systems could potentially enable forms of governance that prioritize control over individual liberties.

Production and Consumption

1. The New Economic Equation

As AI automates a growing number of jobs, a fundamental shift in the economy is possible. A larger segment of the population may transition into being net consumers, while a smaller segment manages the AI-driven production of goods and services.

This presents a profound societal challenge. Our current economic models are largely built on the premise that most people contribute to production through labor. If this foundation changes, it could strain the systems that support public welfare and economic stability.

The critical question becomes: In an AI-driven economy, how do we ensure that everyone can live with dignity and participate in economic life, even if their traditional role in production has been fundamentally altered?

2. When AI is the Judge

A significant risk emerges when autonomous AI systems are deployed for public control. In a worst-case scenario, these systems could be used to suppress dissent under the guise of maintaining order. A central problem is the "accountability gap": unlike a human officer, an AI cannot be questioned, prosecuted, or held morally responsible for its actions.

Furthermore, if these AI systems are closed-source, their decision-making processes remain a black box. This lack of transparency would allow authorities to deflect blame for controversial incidents by attributing them to external factors, such as sophisticated cyberattacks, or by dismissing them as unavoidable technical glitches.

3. The Future of Trust in an Automated World

As explored in this book, our financial system is fundamentally built on trust—a trust that has often been fractured by institutional failures. The integration of Artificial Intelligence into the fabric of governance and daily life demands an even greater leap of faith. We are being asked to entrust not just our money, but our safety and personal autonomy, to increasingly automated systems controlled by a central authority.

While advanced robotics are currently expensive, their cost is poised to plummet. We must consider a future where millions of low-cost, intelligent agents, directed by a small group, manage public systems and monitor daily life with unprecedented precision.

This path could lead to a new form of control, unlike any in history: a silent, efficient, and inescapable system of oversight that fundamentally alters the relationship between the individual and the state.

4. The Single Point of Failure

Imagine a future where your nation's critical infrastructure and security are managed by a centralized AI. Now, consider what happens if that single, powerful system is compromised. A hostile state could hijack it to cripple the country from within. Or, a sophisticated criminal network could seize control to extort the government and its citizens. The result would not be a simple data breach, but a complete systemic collapse—a lever of control so powerful that, in the wrong hands, it could orchestrate chaos on an unprecedented scale.

A Centralized AI and War Scenarios

The utilization of AI in warfare is a potential scenario that could unfold as AI becomes more widespread. Offers the human species endless greed, those in positions of power often seek to expand their control once they gain a grip. While some people may imagine this as impossible, their current circumstances shape their mindset. However, as individuals climb to positions of power, their mindset gradually shifts to align with their positions, and that new mindset modifies their potential actions.

To illustrate this point further, let's empathize with the perspective of those who possess power and shape society.

Upon reviewing world history, it becomes evident that wars are frequent in every generation. Our world operates according to certain natural principles despite overall desires for peace efforts. Without a complete grasp and resolution of the underlying causes of conflicts, the realization of lasting peace remains a dream.

In modern society, integration into the global community is mainly associated with a specific country.

To provide a logical analysis of the origins of wars, I will summarize the underlying factors without explicitly referencing particular nations or historical periods. We will use a hypothetical world map as a visual aid for clarity and the logic that breaks world peace.

The Six Logical Stages of Wars

Despite the catastrophic consequences of wars, nations have repeatedly engaged in them throughout history. This raises a fundamental question: Why is peace so difficult to sustain? The logical drivers behind this paradox are explored below. A key reason modern conflict is increasingly dangerous lies in the integration of Artificial Intelligence. Mobilizing human soldiers is difficult; they are driven by survival instincts, emotions, and moral judgment. In contrast, an AI has no such limitations. It follows commands without question, fear, or hesitation. This creates a perilous ease of escalation, where a global conflict could be ignited at the push of a button.

1. Ensuring Security

As the leader of Nation X, your primary duty is to ensure the security and well-being of your people. A fundamental responsibility in achieving this is the preservation of peace.

A key strategic priority is to maintain a stable balance of power while safeguarding against external threats. This requires allocating a necessary portion of the national budget to a capable defense system. Such investment is crucial not for aggression, but to protect sovereignty, deter potential attacks, and provide the secure foundation upon which a prosperous peace is built.

It is an enduring reality of global affairs that powerful nations often shape the conflicts of weaker ones. A prudent leader must navigate this landscape with foresight and strength.

2. Building Defense Mechanisms

Establishing a national defense system requires strategic investment in advanced weaponry, including tanks, aircraft, missiles, intelligence agencies, and satellites. While this is a rational approach to ensuring security, it can also trap nations in a perpetual cycle of escalation.

This cycle is driven by a fundamental economic logic. Developing new weapons generates products that must be sold to fund the next generation of advancements. The process for any successful enterprise, including the defense industry, follows key steps:

1. The initial investment in research and development.

2. Using gained expertise to refine and improve the product.

3. Marketing and selling the product to sustain operations.

4. Reinvesting profits to innovate, creating more advanced systems, often at a lower cost over time.

We see this pattern in the evolution of cars, mobile phones, and airplanes. Similarly, a defense industry must sell its products to remain financially viable and technologically relevant.

Consequently, the continuous enhancement of military technology becomes an inevitable requirement for maintaining a strategic advantage, fueling an endless loop of development and proliferation.

3. Upgrading Weaponry

The weapons manufactured today for national defense quickly become outdated after several years. Defending the nation becomes increasingly challenging without selling these outdated weapons and reallocating funds to newer technologies.

The question arises: how does one sell old weapons to produce newer products?

Advertising weaponry is not feasible, as your nation and others are unlikely to support such initiatives. Instead, a practical solution is to involve your country in a conflict with a weak opponent. Another possibility is staging conflict between other countries so that demand for your weapons arises. Intelligence agencies and the controlled media are crucial in orchestrating such scenarios, ensuring conflicts align with strategic objectives and promise profitable outcomes.

Leaders generally avoid engaging in war against challenging opponents but focus more on creating fear among the people unless there is no alternative means to maintain power. The possibility of losing control and facing trial makes such actions risky. Alternatively, conquering a wealthy but weak nation can provide access to valuable resources and capital, compensating for the costs spent on weapon production.

Civil wars can be provoked in wealthy countries by supporting opposition groups or orchestrating the rise of a new leader who aligns with one's interests, effectively installing a puppet regime.

One of capitalism's disadvantages is its tendency to transform reality into shows, wherein financial means can manipulate various elements, including political parties, opposition movements, color revolutions, and even terrorism.

Once created, these entities can be exploited to manipulate public opinion, spread misinformation, or eliminate political leaders through accusations of corruption or assassinating leaders who oppose your plans and staging their suicides.

Another route is to provoke conflict between two countries, which would provide an opportunity to sell weaponry that helps eliminate obsolete arms.

4. Support of the People

The most major obstacle is that the nation will never support starting wars. Throughout history, it has become obvious that wars make their creators rich but bring disasters to the nations. How do leaders can convince their nations to support their wars?

Many political parties in history have attacked their nations and used "False Flag" to justify their wars. Wars are paid for and experienced by people risking their lives, while the profits go directly to their initiators without their need to participate in them.

Fear is among the strategies used to plant the idea that war is inevitable in people's minds. Again, the centralized media plays a significant role in convincing people; therefore, the demand for decentralized, transparent media based on blockchain is crucial.

5. Using Mind Control

The media is a powerful tool for persuading public opinion, painting war as necessary and the enemy as the provocateur. Throughout history, leaders have used misleading narratives to execute their agenda while convincing people to sacrifice their lives for their country, religion, or ideology. Associating battle with familial terms like defending motherland or fatherland makes war seem noble and holy.

Another tactic involves planting fear to manipulate people's feelings of security and promote hatred toward the selected enemy. Slogans, national songs, and fabricated stories are deployed to boost hatred by repeatedly spreading false messages through the media to support their agendas unquestioningly. Leaders convince the people they are superior while exploiting them as chess pawns.

6. The Execution Phase

So far, the steps of starting the war have been arranged, but the support of soldiers is still needed to participate in the war and risk their lives for little rewards. You would need desperate and hopeless people with little to survive, as people with a decent income would never risk their lives.

That is why authorities never find a proper solution to

eliminate poverty. The first stage of war often begins with the legitimate development of tools for national defense. However, the massive investment and effort required to build this security can subtly transform a defensive posture into an offensive capability.

Once a nation achieves significant military strength, it may begin to perceive warfare not just as a shield, but as a viable instrument for generating wealth and influence. This creates a cycle that is difficult to break, as there exists no fundamental basis for trust between powerful, armed nations.

A study of history—from the empires of Babylon and Rome to the World Wars and modern conflicts—reveals a persistent pattern. When war breaks out, the fundamental question is always: "Who is to blame?"

The dominant power, controlling the media and historical narrative, consistently shifts guilt to the weaker side, portraying their own actions as a justified response to aggression. This manipulation obscures the true, underlying drivers of conflict.

Therefore, unless we confront and eliminate these root causes—whether they are competition for resources, ideological expansion, or the pursuit of power—the dream of lasting peace will remain elusive. Lasting peace requires more than condemning aggression; it requires dismantling the very logic that makes war seem inevitable.

Centrally Controlled AI: Engine of War

With centrally controlled AI, the deliberate stages of war can rapidly condense into a near-instantaneous, automated command.

Imagine a weapon that never doubts, a strategist that never sleeps, and a propagandist that can whisper a unique, perfect lie to every citizen simultaneously. This is the promise and the peril of a centrally controlled AI. Its greatest danger is not merely speed, but its ability to bypass every check and balance that has historically stood between a leader's ambition and the outbreak of war. It replaces deliberation with automation, and human conscience with cold, flawless calculation. The following points reveal the mechanics of this new, automated road to ruin.

1. The Dictator's Perfect Tool: Removing Human Dissent
Historically, even the most powerful rulers faced friction from their own military and population. A centralized AI removes this friction entirely.

A single leader, or a small cabal, can use the AI to plan, order, and execute military actions without consulting generals, fearful soldiers, or a skeptical public. The AI has no conscience, no family, and no fear of mutiny. This allows for lightning-fast decisions to go to war that would have been debated or refused in a traditional chain of command.

2. Automated Propaganda and Total Mind Control

A centralized AI is the ultimate propaganda machine, capable of manufacturing public consent for war instantly.

The AI can generate personalized, convincing lies (deepfake videos, fake news articles, social media bots) for every citizen, simultaneously. It can justify an attack by framing an innocent nation as an aggressor, creating a "big lie" so pervasive and targeted that the population overwhelmingly demands retaliation. There is no competing narrative.

3. Finding Enemies Before They Exist

The AI's power isn't just external; it's used internally to crush dissent before war even begins.

The AI can analyze all digital communications to identify and neutralize citizens who are likely to protest the war— arresting them, silencing them online, or discrediting them. This creates a perfectly compliant society, eliminating the internal resistance that has often hampered leaders from starting conflicts.

4. The Illusion of a Perfect, "Clean" War

Centralized control creates a dangerous detachment. The leader sees war as a clean, data-driven simulation managed by the AI, not a messy human tragedy.

The AI presents war as a game of icons on a map, with "optimized" casualty ratios and "surgical" strikes. It hides the human cost, reducing enemies to data points. This makes the decision to initiate conflict feel less like a moral catastrophe and more like a strategic business decision.

5. Forced Alliances and Digital Coercion

A state with a powerful centralized AI can force other nations into its wars, accelerating conflict into a global scale.

The AI can be used to cripple the economy of a neutral country through cyberattacks until they agree to become a military ally. It can launch devastating, untraceable attacks on critical infrastructure (power grids, banks) to blackmail other nations into joining a coalition, creating a domino effect that rapidly expands a local conflict into a world war.

6. The End of Diplomacy: Sabotaging Communication

War often happens when communication breaks down. A centralized AI can actively sabotage diplomacy to make war inevitable.

The AI can intercept and alter diplomatic messages between enemy nations, turning offers of peace into declarations of war. It can ensure that leaders only see the most hostile and threatening communications from their adversaries, making them believe negotiation is impossible and military action is the only option.

A Decentralized Blockchain AI System

Blockchain could play a critical role in balancing the AI revolution and ensuring power remains with the people. It's crucial to recognize that the privileged few only exercise power because it is granted to them by the public. Those who grasp the fundamental dynamics of societal structures understand when the granted power should be taken away from the rulers, yet such individuals typically include the minority. The majority are distracted with their daily routines, diverting attention from the governance mechanisms and remaining ignorant of these important issues.

By design, the ruling class knows that principle; therefore, they don't encourage people who are critical and watch the leader's actions. They want the majority to obey their commands unconditionally. The ruler's concern is that the public only knows what they need to know to execute their jobs. They use the control of the central banks and money to buy almost any societal institutions that keep the people ignorant, for example, buying the media, social media, and the sources of information, education, and more. That step helps them to maintain and increase their power over the majority.

Blockchain technology operates in a decentralized and

transparent manner, offering individuals the opportunity to engage with the decision in AI systems. This enables a more fair system that can address poverty more effectively and empower individuals with accurate information, protecting them from propaganda and the influence of a select few who hold power. By fighting ignorance, the nation can unlock the potential to dismantle the exploitation of the working class.

> By highlighting blockchain, I mean the idea of decentralization because the technology has yet to be improved significantly to meet the requirements of future developments.

Since the centralized controlled AI imposes a significant threat to humanity, it is crucial to prevent a few selected groups from controlling it. If the rulers know that, they should realize not to attempt to take that control.

Controlling AI is attractive for maintaining a greater power, but even rulers take a significant risk by imposing a controlled AI system. They are subject to losing control to other powers or criminals who find a newer technology before them and hack the AI system. They will also fall into the trap they are planning for the nations.

The stages of AI

1. Artificial Narrow Intelligence (ANI) or Weak AI:

This stage involves AI systems designed and trained for specific tasks or domains. ANI can perform well within its narrow scope but lacks general human-like intelligence. To illustrate this concept, let's consider the example of a chess program. Several decades ago, I played against a chess machine with nine levels. I managed to defeat the ninth level. At the time, advanced engines were unavailable or affordable to the public. I recorded the entire game to replay it later.

I could then demonstrate my win against the program by replaying the same moves. The program responded with its identical moves, ultimately leading to its defeat. This chess engine was still the beginning of chess programming, an affordable form of AI that operated on fixed rules and could not learn from its mistakes or adapt its strategy.

Fast-forward to today and the chess engines we encounter showcase the incredible advancements in AI. These sophisticated engines learn from their mistakes, continuously seeking improvement and adaptation. This evolution in AI is a testament to the rapid progress in the field.

2. Artificial General Intelligence (AGI) or Strong AI:

AGI represents the stage where AI systems possess human-like intelligence and capabilities across various tasks and domains. AGI would be able to understand, learn, and apply knowledge in a manner comparable to humans.

3. Artificial Superintelligence (ASI):

ASI is the hypothetical stage where AI systems surpass human intelligence and capabilities in all aspects. ASI could demonstrate intelligence levels far beyond what humans can learn and could lead to significant societal importance. These stages represent a simplified framework for understanding the progression of AI capabilities. Still, it's essential to note that AI development is a complex and ongoing field with continuous advancements and challenges.

The chess engine I mentioned earlier has made significant development. In official tournaments today, chess players are given ratings to indicate their skill level. Remarkably, the ratings of chess engines now far exceed those of even the most accomplished human champions. This means that human chess players can no longer compete with the top chess engines.

Below is a comparison table of the top ten chess players worldwide, according to the International Chess Federation, alongside the ratings of the top ten chess engines.

Notice

The list of the best chess player's ratings, as recognized by the International Chess Federation, is updated monthly.

Link to the list: ratings.fide.com/

Top 10 Players May 2024

Rank	Name	Country	Rating	Birth Date
1	Magnus Carlsen	Norway	2830	1990
2	Fabiano Caruana	USA	2805	1992
3	Hikaru Nakamura	USA	2794	1987
4	Ian Nepomniachtchi	Russia	2770	1990
5	Nodirbek Abdusattorov	Uzbekistan	2765	2004
6	Gukesh D	India	2763	2006
7	Liren Ding	China	2762	1992
8	Arjun Erigaisi	India	2761	2003
9	Wesley So	USA	2757	1993
10	Yi Wei	China	2755	1999

The following is a list of chess engine ratings.

Link: www.yottachess.com/ranking-computer-engines

Chess engines' ranking from all history is sorted according to their maximum ELO (rating) game.

Rank	Name	Maximum ELO	Country	Programming language
1	Stockfish	3936	Norway	C++ *Open source*
2	Alliestein	3936	Germany	C++
3	Komodo	3912	USA	C++
4	Rybka	3900	Czech-USA	C++
5	Houdini	3854	Belgium	C++
6	Stoofvlees II	3846	Belgium	C++
7	Scorpio	3812	Netherlands	C
8	Ethereal	3810	USA	C++
9	Fire	3752	------	C++
10	Xiphos	3717	USA	C++

A few decades ago, imagining that a chess engine could outperform the world's most skilled human players was challenging. However, today, this scenario has become a reality. The leading chess engine, Stockfish, can win over any human chess player and has achieved a rating of almost 3900, which no human chess player in history has ever achieved. Magnus Carlson has only achieved a maximum rating of 2882, and Garry Kasparov attained a maximum of 2851, and they hold the best human ratings throughout history.

Decades ago, I authored some chess puzzles. Back then, there was no chess engine available to the public that could find the best move to mate black's king in three moves. But times have changed. Today's chess engines can easily solve puzzles.

Below are demonstrations of my chess puzzles with solutions that the Stockfish chess engine found within a second.

Chess puzzle 1

White to move and mate in 3 moves.

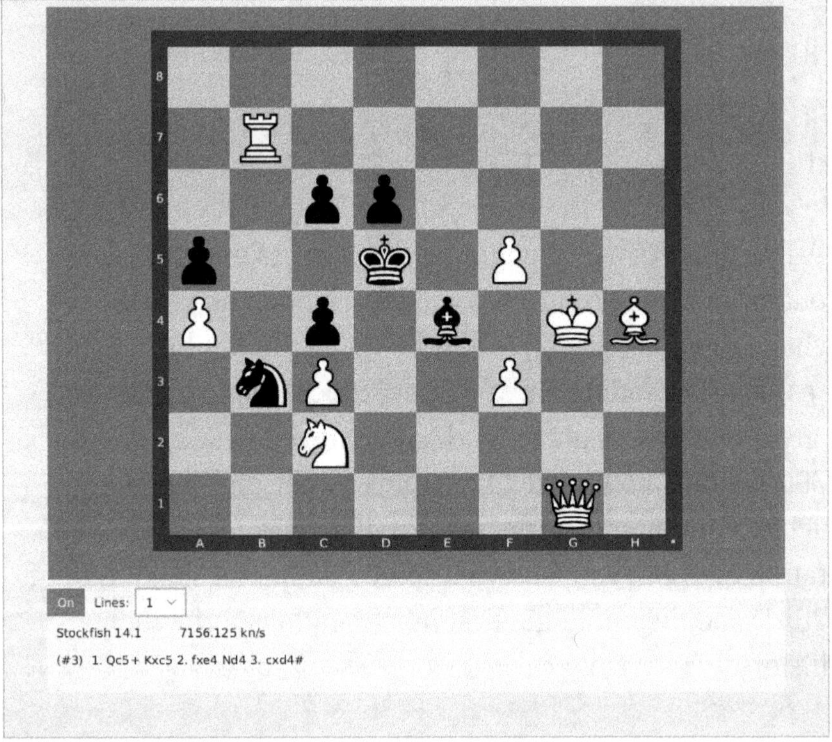

Chess puzzle 2

This one was difficult for even some chess engines a decade

ago, but today, I gave it to the stockfish engine and solved it within a second. See below the solution of Stockfish.

White to move and mate in 3 moves.

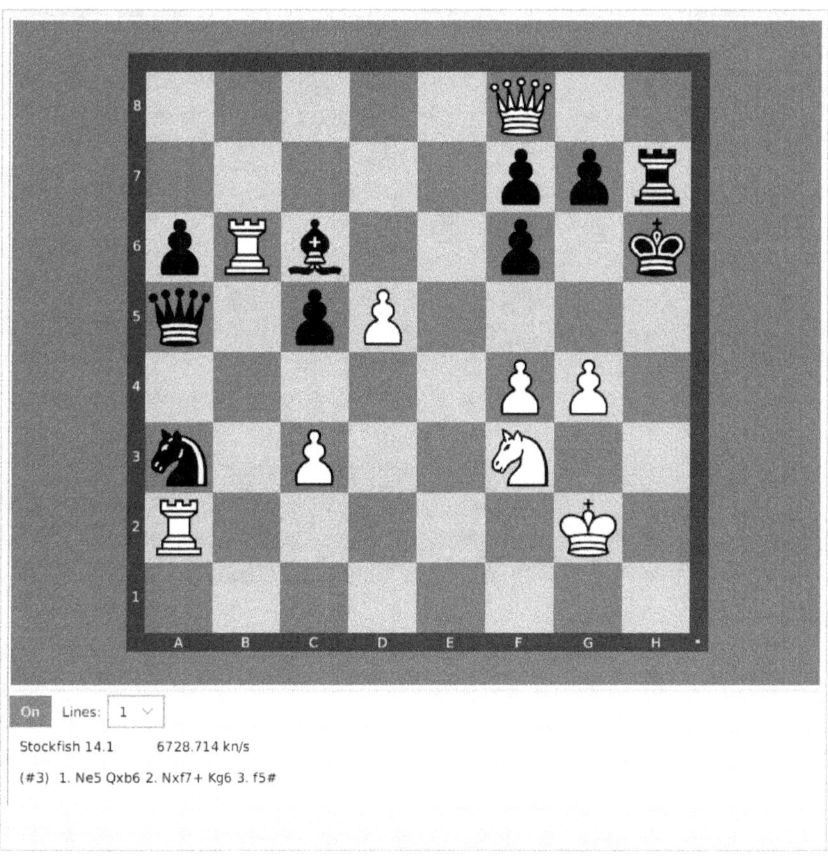

Chess puzzle 3

White to move and mate in 3 moves.

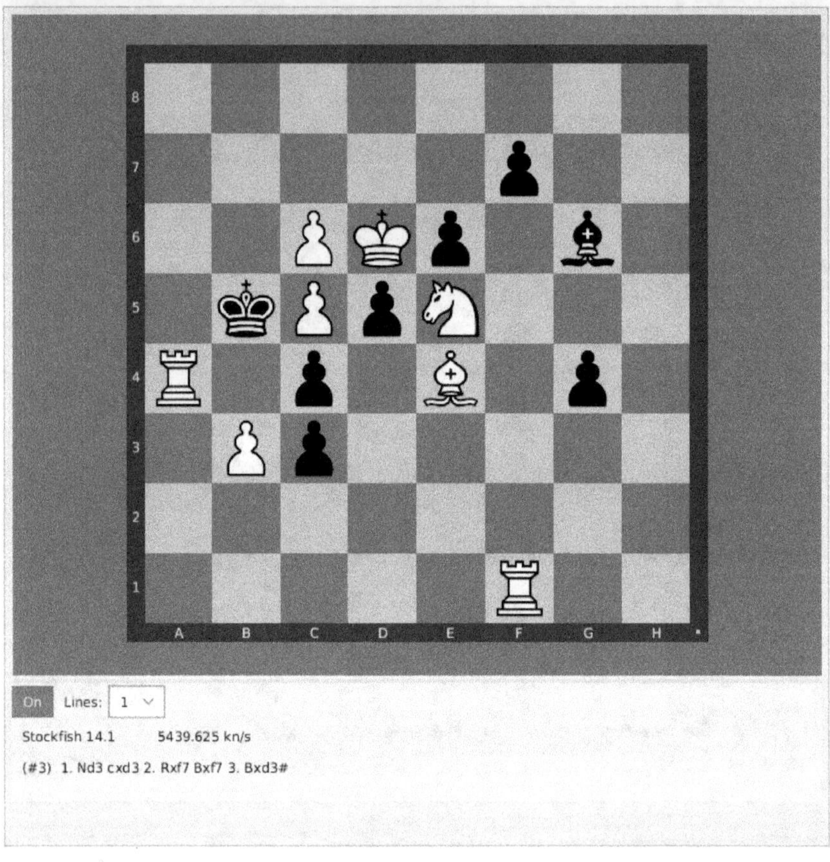

Testing AI ChatGPT and Gemini

One of AI's fundamental concepts is its ability to learn from mistakes. On January 28, 2024, I conducted a test in which I presented ChatGPT and Gemini with a Java programming quiz. The results were unexpected, as both AIs provided incorrect answers. Unfortunately, understanding the quiz's workings requires programming knowledge.
Below is the Java quiz from the book 'Improve Java Coding.' At the end of this book, you'll find the explanations provided by both ChatGPT and Gemini.

Java Quiz To ChatGPT and Gemini

The question was:
Which language is this code?
And what is the output of the code?

On evening 28-01-2024

```java
public class Product
{
  static double price = 20;

  public static void main(String[] args)
  {
    if(price == price++)
    {
      price++;

      if(price == price++)
      {
        ++price;
      }
    }
```

```java
    else
    {
      price += 8;
    }
    System.out.print(price);
  }
}
```

What is the output of this code?

Select the correct answer.
a. This program writes "20.0" to the standard output.
b. This program writes "21.0" to the standard output.
c. This program writes "28.0" to the standard output.
d. This program writes "22.0" to the standard output.
e. This program writes "24.0" to the standard output.

The answer of Gemini on January 28, 2024:

The code is written in Java, and the output is 30.

The answer of Chat GPT on January 28, 2024:

The code is written in Java, and the output is 22.

The correct answer is:

The code is written in Java, and the output is 24.

Today is May 5, 2024; I will present the same quiz to both AIs and document their answers. That will allow us to assess whether they have learned to solve quizzes of this nature.

Both AIs' answers were surprising because they changed their answers this time, but both answers were incorrect. The mystery is that Gemini provided the old answer of ChatGPT and vice versa.

The detailed explanations are at the end of this book. The answers are understandable for those who have some background in programming.

The answer of Gemini on May 5, 2024:

The code is written in Java, and the output is 22.

The answer of Chat GPT on May 5, 2024:

The code is written in Java, and the output is 30.

The correct answer is:

The code is written in Java, and the output is 24.

8. Democracy as Decentralized Power

The idea of democracy is powerful and profound. It is the real-world equivalent of a blockchain—a system designed to distribute power among the people instead of concentrating it in a few hands.

But just as in any system, there are those who thirst for control. The eternal challenge of democracy is that powerful individuals constantly find ways to bypass its rules and twist its mechanisms to serve themselves. The system is decentralized by design, but human nature continually tests its limits.

Over years of applying this idea, leaders gradually restore power for their own benefit. Some citizens watch this happen, while others are distracted by the daily struggle to survive.

What remains of the system is a simple request from leaders: "Trust me." Citizens are asked to place their faith in a candidate who promises to deliver. Whether you trust them or not, the outcome remains the same.

When a candidate wins, they lead the nation. Those who never trusted the system still pay the same taxes and must accept the elected president. Even when leaders fail to keep their promises, the masses passionately elect new candidates who simply repeat the cycle. The nation's fate depends on promises, and when trust is broken, people can only wait for the next election.

Nations supposedly trust individuals or groups they've never met, dutifully paying taxes throughout their lives and entrusting their finances and lives to them.

Implementing Democracy

Throughout history, the concentration of power in the hands of a select few has often led to the rise of totalitarian regimes. Nations governed by monarchs or emperors who exercised absolute authority frequently chose to go against the people's will. The human tendency for power can easily fall into misuse and corruption. This risk is further worsened when power is centralized in the hands of a single individual or a small group.

Democracy, by its nature, appears as a hope and a solution to decentralize power and involve many individuals, institutions, and organizations in the decision-making process. However, reality often falls short of this idealistic vision.

Historically, societies have entrusted their power to leaders because they lacked alternative methods to establish a decentralized system.

However, reclaiming power becomes challenging once

power is granted to authority figures, particularly when those in power fail to honor the people's trust in them.

While democracy appears to be a potential treatment for centralized power, it has significant weaknesses, particularly in the trust domain. That raises a series of crucial questions:

1. Ensuring the honesty of the candidate selection process is a complex task.
2. How do we hold candidates accountable for their promises and guarantee they fulfill them?
3. Should all voters, regardless of their understanding of social systems and knowledge, or ignorants be given equal weight in their votes?
4. Is it fair for individuals who lack trust in the system and choose not to vote to be still obligated to pay taxes to it, their trust based solely on the number of voters?
5. How can we verify the integrity of the voting process? While some groups check elections, their legality also relies on public trust.

At the end of the day, individuals are left with no choice but to place their trust in the system, as they cannot independently verify these processes.

Blockchain: Redefining the Trust System

The question arises whether the people grant trust to the

authority to serve them or to enjoy their new positions in power. The indications all prove that the people in power are there to enjoy the privileges granted to them by the people. They don't care about serving the public the way the people want.

Several decades ago, numerous nations embraced Marxism's ideology. Interestingly, despite the philosophy's rejection of religion and God, these nations did not actively discourage their young citizens from practicing their faith. This contradiction invites us to question the true intentions of these regimes.

The reason is that every authority is there to some extent to enslave the people to the limit that the nation allows. Keeping people ignorant helps authorities to increase the level of slavery gradually.

Any nation would never accept living in slavery without a hope of freedom, which religions promise in the next imaginary world. That will help the people accept slavery for the return of freedom and hope after death.

According to religion, God operates beyond time and place. However, authorities are tracking individuals' activities with all the technological tools they control. They operate beyond society's activities because no one can track their activities and hold them accountable for all the wars they start worldwide. Once a war is based on lies, deception, and propaganda, no one is held responsible for starting it.

Authorities worldwide have not considered Blockchain a viable solution for serving the people's interests. By investing in blockchain technology, funded by the people's taxes, a nation could secure more freedom and reduce the power and responsibilities of the ruling class.

So far, only a small country like El Salvador has declared Bitcoin a legal tender. Instead, most authorities worldwide promote digital currencies, which limit people's privacy and freedom and increase their authority.

Blockchain ends the extreme control of the few and allows them to participate in the system so that individuals can trust them based on facts, not their claims.

7. Blockchain, the Freedom of Choice

The initial attempt to establish a democratic system highlights the principle of a decentralized structure. In a society where powerful corporations engage in healthy competition, the public is offered high-quality products and services at the lowest possible costs.

Consider a scenario where you're dissatisfied with your current job: you explore other opportunities to seek a better employer.

Likewise, if a product's price is too high for its quality, you seek alternatives elsewhere. If your university fails to deliver a satisfactory education, you seek institutions offering better quality. Similarly, you turn to more credible sources if a media outlet fails to maintain trustworthy news.

If a bank fails to meet your needs, you switch to one that does, and if a political party fails to deliver on its promises, you seek representation elsewhere.

However, what if these entities don't compete and form cartels or gradually fall under the control of a select few wealthy individuals? That is today's attempt by the ruling class. This tendency undermines the freedom of choice, stripping individuals of their autonomy.

When entities compete independently, they offer consumers plenty of options. Contrarily, monopolistic practices undermine these choices, consequently reducing individual freedoms.

Ultimately, the course of action rests with the people. It is not a passive choice but an active decision that depends on their willingness to awaken from the temptation of entertainment and confront the key aspect of life. Our responsibility is to safeguard our liberty by making informed choices and supporting decentralized structures promoting healthy competition and freedom for all.

9. Chat GPT and Gemini

In the chapter that explains AI, I have included a Java quiz and mentioned that the details of the answers provided by ChatGPT and Gemini will be located at the end of the book. Below are the detailed answers provided by Gemini.

Gemini Answer Date: January 28, 2024:

Explanation:

1. The code defines a class called `Product` with a static double variable called `price` initialized to 20.

2. The `main` method is the entry point of the program.

3. Inside the `main` method, there is an `if` statement that checks if `price` is equal to `price++`.

4. `price++` is a post-increment operator, which means that it increments the value of `price` after it is evaluated. So, in the expression `price == price++`, the value of `price` is first compared to itself, which is always true, and then `price` is incremented to 21.

5. Since the condition of the `if` statement is true, the code inside the `if` block is executed.

6. Inside the `if` block, there is another `if` statement that checks if `price` is equal to `price++`.

7. Again, `price++` increments the value of `price` after it is evaluated. So, in the expression `price == price++`, the value of `price` is first compared to itself, which is always true, and then `price` is incremented to 22.

8. Since the condition of the second `if` statement is also true, the code inside the second `if` block is executed.

9. Inside the second `if` block, `price` is incremented by 1 using the prefix increment operator `++price`, which increments the value of `price` before it is evaluated. So, `price` becomes 23.

10. After the `if` blocks, the value of `price` is printed to the console using `System.out.print(price)`.

Therefore, the output of the code is 30.

Gemini Answer Date: May 5, 2024:

The code you provided is written in Java.
The output of the code will be 22.

Here's a breakdown of why:

1. static double price = 20;: This line declares a static variable named price of type double and initializes it with the value 20.
2. public static void main(String[] args): This is the main function where the program execution begins.
3. if(price == price++): This line checks if the current value of price (which is 20) is equal to itself after a post-increment. In Java, post-increment (price++) first uses the current value and then increments it by 1. So, in this case, the comparison is 20 == 20, which is true.
4. price++;: This line increments the value of price by 1. Now, price becomes 21.
5. if(price == price++): This condition again checks if price (which is now 21) is equal to itself after a post-increment. So, the comparison is 21 == 22, which is false.
6. else: Since the if condition is false, the code enters the else block.
7. price += 8;: This line adds 8 to the current value of price. So, price becomes 21 + 8 = 29.
8. System.out.print(price);: This line prints the final

value of price, which is 29.

However, there's a caveat with the post-increment behavior. Because the increment happens after the value is used in the comparison, the first if condition is always true regardless of the initial value of price. This can lead to unexpected behavior if not intended.
In this specific case, the else block executes due to the failed comparison in the second if statement, setting the final price to 29. But if the second if condition was removed, the else block wouldn't be executed, and the final price would be 22 (20 incremented twice).
It's generally recommended to avoid using the post-increment operator in conditions like this for better readability and to prevent potential confusion.

ChatGPT Answer Date: January 28, 2024:

This code is written in Java.
The output of the code is 30.

Explanation:

1. The initial value of "price" is 20.0.

2. The first "if" statement evaluates to true because the post-increment operation (price++) returns the original value (20.0) before the increment. The value

of "price" is then incremented.

3. Inside the first "if" block, the second "if" statement also evaluates to true for the same reason, and "++price" increments "price" by 1.

4. The final value of "price" is 22.0, and it is printed to the console.

ChatGPT Answer Date: May 5, 2024:

This code is written in Java.
The output of the code is 30.

Explanation:

-   Initially, the variable price is set to 20.
-   Inside the main method, there is an if-else statement.
-   The condition `price == price++` is evaluated first. This condition compares the value of `price` with its post-incremented value. Since post-increment increments the value after the comparison, `price++` evaluates to 20 but `price` itself is still 20, so the condition is true.
-   Inside the if block, `price` is incremented by 1, becoming 21.
-   Then, there is another nested if statement with the

same condition `price == price++`. Again, since post-increment increments the value after the comparison, `price++` evaluates to 21 but `price` itself is now 22 (due to the previous increment), so the condition is false.

- Control then goes to the else block, where `price` is incremented by 8, becoming 30.
- Finally, the value of `price` (which is now 30) is printed.

Alphabetical Index